Bon Appetit

SALADS

Foreword

Crisp, fresh salads using lettuce, vegetables or fruit are always nutritious and enjoyable. This book contains a great variety of salads as well as sweet and savoury dressings and sauces

Do be careful to follow one type of measure throughout the recipe. The three measurements given are Metric, Imperial and American (cups). Where American ingredients differ from English, the American name has been put in brackets.

All recipes are for four people unless otherwise stated.

Bon Appétit.

California salad

Ingredients

For the salad
½ iceberg lettuce, washed,
trimmed, leaves separated
1 small honeydew melon
3 oranges, peeled
3 carrots
100g/4oz/¼ lb peas, shelled

For the dressing
150ml/¼ pt/⅔ cup yoghurt
2x15ml/2tbs/3tbs soured cream
1x15ml/1tbs/2tbs lemon juice
1x15ml/1tbs/2tbs orange juice

salt
freshly ground white pepper
hazelnuts, ground
tarragon, spray

Method

Cut the melon in half, remove the seeds and scoop the fruit out with a parisienne cutter. Remove the pith, pips and skin from the oranges and divide into segments, retaining the juice. Clean and slice the carrots. Put the peas and carrots into a little boiling, salted water. Boil for 5 minutes, drain and cool.
Put the salad ingredient into bowls or hollowed out halves of melon.
Mix the yoghurt and soured cream together with the lemon and orange juice. Season. Pour the dressing over the salad, sprinkle with hazelnuts and garnish with tarragon. Serve at once.

Chicory salad with horseradish

Ingredients

For the salad
350g/12oz/¾ lb chicory
2 apples, large dessert
100g/4oz/¼ lb ham, sliced

For the dressing
50g/2oz/4tbs horseradish, grated
6x15ml/6tbs/8tbs double cream
(heavy cream)
1x15ml/1tbs/2tbs white wine
vinegar
salt

Method

Remove the outermost leaves from the chicory. Cut in half and remove the hard core. Wash, drain and slice. Peel, quarter, core and slice the apples. Chop the ham.
Mix the horseradish into the cream, add the vinegar. Season with salt. Pour the dressing over the salad, toss lightly.

Crispy leaf salads

Spinach salad with oranges

Ingredients

For the salad
*225g/8oz/½ lb spinach, well
washed, spines removed,
drained*

For the dressing
*½ an orange
2x15ml/2tbs/3tbs lemon juice
3x15ml/3tbs/4tbs salad oil
salt and pepper
castor sugar (fine granulated)
chopped thyme*

Method

Peel the orange very thinly, cut the rind into narrow strips. Boil the
rind in a little water for 3 minutes, cool. Stir the lemon juice and
oil, add the thyme. Season with salt, pepper and sugar. Remove the
pith and outer skin from the orange and cut the fruit into cubes.
Stir into the sauce with the rind. Pour the sauce over the salad,
toss lightly.

Radicchio with lamb's lettuce

(illustrated pages 8-9)

Ingredients

For the salad
*100g/4oz/¼ lb radicchio
(Italian red lettuce)
100g/4oz/ ¼ lb lamb's lettuce
(corn salad)*

For the dressing
*1 onion, peeled, finely chopped
5x15ml/5tbs/6tbs salad oil
2x15ml/2tbs/3tbs vinegar
1x5ml/1tsp/1tsp mustard
salt and pepper
castor sugar (fine granulated)
1x15ml/1tbs/2tbs parsley,
chopped
1x15ml/1tbs/2tbs chives,
chopped
1 hardboiled egg, shelled*

Method

Cut off the root ends from the radicchio, discard any wilted leaves and then pick off the rest (tear largest leaves into small pieces). Trim root ends from corn salad (lamb's lettuce). Wash these two ingredients thoroughly and leave to drain.
Mix the onion with the oil, vinegar and mustard. Season with salt, pepper, sugar, parsley and chives. Pour the dressing over the salad. Garnish with slices of egg and serve immediately.

Savoury Chinese cabbage salad

Ingredients

For the salad
500g/1lb/1lb Chinese cabbage
For the dressing
1 small onion, peeled, finely
chopped
3x15ml/3tbs/4tbs salad oil
1x15ml/1tbs/2tbs vinegar
2x15ml/2tbs/3tbs tomato
ketchup (catsup)
1x5ml/1tsp/1tsp mustard
1x5ml/1tsp/1tsp castor sugar
(fine granulated)
salt and pepper

Method

Remove the outermost leaves and cut the cabbage in half. Cut into narrow strips, then wash and drain well.
Stir the onion with the oil, vinegar, tomato ketchup, mustard and sugar. Season. Pour the dressing over the cabbage and toss. Serve at once.

Watercress salad

Ingredients

For the salad
100g/4oz/¼ lb watercress

For the dressing
1 small onion or 5 shallots
3x15ml/3tbs/4tbs salad oil

1x15ml/1tbs/2tbs vinegar
salt and pepper
castor sugar (fine granulated)
2x15ml/2tbs/3tbs mixed herbs,
chopped
2 hardboiled eggs, shelled

Method

Trim the watercress and drain well.
Peel and halve the shallots or onion, slice and mix with the oil and vinegar. Season with salt, pepper and sugar. Stir in the herbs. Pour the dressing over the watercress, toss lightly. Chop the egg and sprinkle over the salad. Serve at once.

Iceberg salad

(facing page)

Ingredients

For the salad
1 iceberg lettuce, washed,
trimmed, leaves separated
2 oranges, peeled, segmented

For the dressing
150ml/¼ pt/⅔ cup yoghurt
1x5ml/1tsp/1tsp salad oil
2x15ml/2tbs/3tbs vinegar
salt
castor sugar (fine granulated)

Method

Mix together the yoghurt and salad oil, stir in the vinegar. Season with salt and sugar. Pour the dressing over the salad ingredients and toss lightly.

Iceberg salad with kiwifruit

(4 - 6 portions)

Ingredients

For the salad
*1 iceberg lettuce, washed,
trimmed, leaves separated
3 courgettes (zucchini)
3 kiwifruit, peeled
2 sticks celery
100g/4oz/¼ lb best ham*

For the dressing
*3x15ml/3tbs/4tbs salad oil
1x15ml/1tbs/2tbs lemon juice
salt and pepper
castor sugar (fine granulated)
1x15ml/1tbs/2tbs tarragon,
chopped
50g/2oz/4tbs pistachio nuts,
blanched, skinned, chopped*

Method

Cut the tips off the courgettes. Slice the kiwifruit and courgettes.
Remove any tough fibres from the celery, slice thinly. Cut the ham
into strips.
Mix the oil and lemon juice, season with salt, pepper and sugar.
Stir in tarragon. Pour the dressing over the salad, sprinkle with the
pistachio nuts.

Nut and apple salad

Ingredients

For the salad
*2 lettuces, washed, trimmed,
leaves separated
2 sour apples, peeled, cored
2x15ml/2tbs/3tbs lemon juice*

For the dressing
*2x15ml/2tbs/3tbs walnut oil
1x15ml/1tbs/2tbs white wine
vinegar
2x5ml/2tsp/3tsp orange juice
salt and white pepper
2x15ml/2tbs/3tbs walnuts,
roughly chopped*

14

Method

Cut the apple into quarters, then slice. Sprinkle with lemon juice.
Mix the walnut oil and vinegar, stir in the orange juice, season.
Mix the dressing with the salad ingredients and sprinkle with
walnuts. Serve at once.

Nut and apple salad

Spanish salad

(6-8 portions)

Ingredients

5 tomatoes, blanched, skinned
½ cucumber
3 peppers, halved
2 red onions, peeled
1 lettuce, trimmed, rinsed

Garnish
1 hardboiled egg, sliced
stuffed olives
strips red pepper

For the dressing
3x15ml/3tbs/4tbs olive oil
1x15ml/1tbs/2tbs wine vinegar
salt and pepper
castor sugar (fine granulated)
2x15ml/2tbs/3tbs parsley,
chopped

Method

Slice the tomatoes and cucumber. Remove the stalks, seeds and ribs
from the peppers, rinse and cut into strips. Cut the onion into
rings.
Mix the oil and vinegar, season with salt, pepper and sugar and stir
in the parsley. Mix the dressing into the salad. Check the seasoning
and garnish with egg, olives and red pepper.

Radicchio asparagus salad

Ingredients

For the salad
500g/1lb/1lb asparagus, trimmed,
rinsed, lightly peeled
275g/10oz/10oz radicchio
(Italian red lettuce)
1 red onion, peeled
100g/4oz/ ¼ lb mushrooms

For the dressing
3x15ml/3tbs/4tbs olive oil
3x15ml/3tbs/4tbs lemon juice
salt and pepper
dill, chopped

Method

Put the asparagus into 500ml/18fl oz/2 ¼ cups boiling, salted water. Bring back to the boil and boil for 5 minutes. Drain and rinse the asparagus under cold, running water. Leave to drain. Cut the root ends off the radicchio, discard any wilted leaves, separate the rest and tear the larger ones in half. Wash thoroughly and leave to drain. Halve the onion and cut into thin slices. Wash and thinly slice the mushrooms.
Mix the oil with the lemon juice. Season. Pour over the salad, toss well and sprinkle with dill.

Radicchio asparagus salad

Bulgarian endive salad

Ingredients

For the salad
1 large endive, trimmed,
rinsed
75g/3oz/6tbs goats cheese

For the dressing
2x15ml/2tbs/3tbs salad oil
1x15ml/1tbs/2tbs wine vinegar
3x15ml/3tbs/4tbs soured cream
3x15ml/3tbs/4tbs yoghurt
salt and pepper
cayenne pepper
2x15ml/2tbs/3tbs chives, finely
chopped
basil, chopped

Method

Separate the endive leaves, crumble the cheese and toss gently together.
Stir the oil into the vinegar and add the soured cream and yoghurt.
Season with salt, pepper and cayenne. Stir in the chives and basil.
Pour the dressing over the salad.

Endive apple salad

Ingredients

For the salad
1 endive, trimmed, rinsed
2 sour apples, peeled, cored

For the dressing
5x15ml/5tbs/6tbs salad oil
2x15ml/2tbs/3tbs herb vinegar
salt
freshly ground white pepper
castor sugar (fine granulated)

Method

Quarter the apples and slice thinly.
Mix the oil with the vinegar, season with salt, pepper and sugar.
Mix the dressing with the salad and serve at once.

Basic lettuce salad

Ingredients

For the salad
2 lettuces, washed, trimmed, leaves separated

For the dressing
3x15ml/3tbs/4tbs salad oil
1x15ml/1tbs/2tbs vinegar

salt and pepper
castor sugar (fine granulated)
1x15ml/1tbs/2tbs herbs,
chopped (dill, chives, parsley
tarragon, chervil, watercress)

Method

Stir the vinegar into the salad oil. Season with salt, pepper and sugar. Stir in the herbs.
Variation: Add 1-2 medium-sized onions, peeled and chopped.
Mix the dressing into the lettuce just before serving, toss lightly.

Endive apple salad   *Bulgarian endive salad*

Salad with walnut dressing

Ingredients

For the salad
2 lettuces, trimmed, rinsed,
leaves separated

For the dressing
1 small red onion, peeled
3x15ml/3tbs/4tbs walnut oil

1x15ml/1tbs/2tbs white wine
vinegar
50g/2oz/4tbs walnuts, coarsely
chopped
salt and pepper
castor sugar (fine granulated)

Method
Finely slice the onion, mix with the oil, vinegar and walnuts.
Season with salt, pepper and sugar. Mix the dressing with the
lettuce. Check the seasoning and serve at once.

Summer salad

(facing page)

Ingredients

For the salad
1 lettuce, trimmed, rinsed,
leaves separated
1 bunch radishes
½ cucumber
20 stuffed olives

For the dressing
50g/2oz/2oz Danish Blue

cheese
2x15ml/2tbs/3tbs soured cream
3x15ml/3tbs/4tbs olive oil
2x15ml/2tbs/3tbs wine vinegar
freshly ground black pepper
castor sugar (fine granulated)
1x15ml/1tbs/2tbs herbs,
chopped
(parsley, tarragon, sorrel)

Method
Wash the radishes and quarter lengthways. Wash the cucumber and
cut in half lengthways. Remove the seeds and cut in 5cm/2" strips.
Chop half the olives finely, halve the rest. (The finely chopped
olives are for the dressing.)
Rub the cheese through a sieve, stir in the soured cream, oil and
vinegar. Season with pepper and sugar. Add the chopped olives and
stir in the herbs. Pour the dressing over the salad and serve at once.

Iceberg salad Gisela

Ingredients

For the salad
½ iceberg lettuce, trimmed,
rinsed, torn into pieces
1x15ml/1tbs/2tbs lemon juice
1 sour apple, peeled, cored
1 leek - white part only
100g/4oz/¼ lb boiled ham
150g/5oz/5oz mushrooms

For the dressing
4x15ml/4tbs/5tbs salad oil
3x15ml/3tbs/4tbs herb vinegar
salt and pepper
castor sugar (fine granulated)
2x15ml/2tbs/3tbs herbs,
chopped
(parsley, chervil, dill, lemon
balm)
Garnish
hardboiled egg, sliced

Method

Wash and thinly slice the mushrooms. Sprinkle with lemon juice.
Quarter the apple, then slice and add to the mushrooms. Cut the
leek in half lenghtways, then slice thinly. Wash and drain. Cut ham
into strips.
Stir the oil with the vinegar, season with salt, pepper and sugar.
Stir in the herbs. Mix the dressing with the salad (omit the lettuce).
Leave for about 10 minutes, then add the lettuce and toss well.
Check seasoning. Garnish with slices of egg.

Sweetcorn salad

(facing page)

Ingredients

For the salad
1 lettuce, trimmed, rinsed,
leaves separated
1 yellow pepper, halved
225g/8oz/½ lb canned
sweetcorn

For the dressing
4x15ml/4tbs/5tbs olive oil
2x15ml/2tbs/3tbs red wine

vinegar
1 clove garlic, peeled, crushed
1 x 2.5 ml/ ½ tsp/ ½ tsp castor
sugar (fine granulated)
1x5ml/1tsp/1tsp mustard
a pinch of chives, basil,
marjoram, lovage, chopped
1 hardboiled egg, shelled
parsley, chopped

Method

Remove the stem, seeds and ribs of the yellow pepper. Wash and cut into thin strips. Drain the sweetcorn.

Mix together the oil, vinegar, garlic, sugar and mustard. Stir in the herbs (omit the parsley). Chop the egg finely and add to the other ingredients. Mix the dressing with the salad. Sprinkle with parsley.

Chicory salad with cheese dressing

Ingredients

For the salad
500g/1lb/1lb chicory

For the dressing
50g/2oz/4tbs cottage cheese, sieved
3x15ml/3tbs/4tbs salad oil
1x15ml/1tbs/2tbs wine vinegar
salt
sugar

Method

Discard the outermost leaves of the chicory. Cut in half and
remove the hard central core. Wash, leave to drain, slice. Mix
together the cottage cheese, oil and vinegar. Season with salt and
sugar. Mix the dressing with the salad. Add salt, sugar and vinegar
to taste. Serve at once.

Iceberg salad with fruit

Ingredients

For the salad
iceberg lettuce, trimmed, rinsed, torn into pieces
1 grapefruit, peeled
1 orange, peeled
2 kiwifruit, peeled, sliced

For the dressing
4x15ml/4tbs/5tbs salad oil

2x15ml/2tbs/3tbs lemon juice
1x15ml/1tbs/2tbs vinegar
2x15ml/2tbs/3tbs castor sugar (fine granulated)
50g/2oz/4tbs walnuts, chopped
salt and pepper

Garnish
walnuts, halved

Method

Cut the grapefruit and orange in half and slice. Put all the salad ingredients into a bowl.
Mix together the oil, lemon juice, vinegar, sugar and chopped walnuts. Season. Pour the dressing over the salad. Garnish with halved walnuts and serve at once.

Iceberg salad with fruit

Winter salad

Ingredients

For the salad
300g/10oz/10oz radicchio
(Italian red lettuce)
100g/4oz/¼ lb endive

For the dressing
5x15ml/5tbs/6tbs salad oil
2x15ml/2tbs/3tbs freshly
squeezed orange juice
salt
freshly ground pepper
2 red onions, peeled
castor sugar (fine granulated)

Method

Trim and rinse the radicchio and endive. Separate the leaves, shake dry.
Stir together the oil and orange juice. Season with salt, pepper and sugar. Cut the onion into thin slices and add to the dressing. Leave to marinate for about 30 minutes, turning occasionally. Mix the dressing with the salad. Check seasoning. Serve at once with rye bread and butter.

Salad with cream cheese dressing

(facing page)

Ingredients

For the salad
1 cos lettuce, trimmed, rinsed
1 bunch radishes, sliced
2 large tomatoes, blanched,
peeled, seeded
1 red onion, peeled, halved,
sliced
100g/4oz/¼ lb mushrooms,
sliced
3 sticks celery

For the dressing
2x15ml/2tbs/3tbs salad oil
3x15ml/3tbs/4tbs wine vinegar
salt and pepper
castor sugar (fine granulated)
50g/2oz/4tbs herb cream cheese
150ml/¼ pt/⅔ cup soured cream
2x15ml/2tbs/3tbs parsley,
chopped

Method

Break up the lettuce leaves. Cut the tomatoes into 8 sections.
Remove any tough fibres from the celery, cut into fine slices.
Mix the oil with the vinegar. Season with salt, pepper and sugar
and pour over the salad. Toss well. Mash the herb cream cheese
with a fork and then stir in the soured cream. Season, add the
parsley and either spoon over the salad or serve separately.

Endive and mushroom salad

Ingredients

For the salad
1 endive, trimmed, rinsed,
shaken dry
3 stalks celery
175g/6oz/6oz mushrooms

For the dressing
8 anchovy fillets, soaked
in milk
3x15ml/3tbs/4tbs salad oil
1x15ml/1tbs/2tbs wine vinegar
1x15ml/1tbs/2tbs double cream
(heavy cream)
1x15ml/1tbs/2tbs hazelnuts,
ground (filberts)
pepper
castor sugar (fine granulated)

Method

Cut the endive into strips. Remove any tough fibres from the
celery, wash and slice. Wash and slice the mushrooms.
Dry the anchovies and finely mash half. Mix together with the oil,
vinegar, cream, hazelnuts. Season with pepper and sugar. Mix the
dressing with the salad ingredients. Garnish with remaining
anchovies.

Spanish endive and pepper salad

Ingredients

For the salad
1 endive, trimmed, rinsed,
2 red peppers, halved
10 stuffed olives

For the dressing
1 onion, peeled
1 hardboiled egg, shelled
4 x 15 ml/4 tbs/5 tbs olive oil
3 x 15 ml/3 tbs/4 tbs white wine
vinegar
salt and pepper

castor sugar *(fine granulated)*
mustard
paprika

Method

Cut the endive in half, slice in strips. Remove stems, seeds and ribs
of peppers. Wash and slice. Slice the olives.
Finely chop the onion. Remove the yolk from the egg and mash
finely. Chop the egg white and set aside. Mix the oil with the
vinegar, onion and egg yolk. Season with salt, pepper, sugar,
mustard and paprika. Mix the dressing with the salad, sprinkle with
the egg white. Serve at once.

Tip: Cut a French bread lengthways and spread with garlic butter.
Wrap in aluminium foil and put it in the oven for a short while
(225°C/450°F/Gas 6-7). Slice the bread and serve while still warm.

Endive and mushroom salad   *Spanish endive and pepper salad*

Chinese cabbage salad

Ingredients

For the salad
500g/1lb/1lb Chinese cabbage

For the dressing
4x15ml/4tbs/5tbs double cream
(heavy cream)
salt and pepper
1x15ml/1tbs/2tbs wine vinegar
castor sugar (fine granulated)
2x15ml/2tbs/3tbs mixed herbs,
chopped

Method

Discard the outermost leaves from the Chinese cabbage. Cut in half and shred finely.
Mix the cream, salt, pepper, vinegar and sugar. Stir in the herbs.
Toss the dressing with the salad and chill for 10 minutes.

Spinach salad

Ingredients

For the salad
225g/8oz/½ lb spinach
5 tomatoes
3 hardboiled eggs, shelled

For the dressing
1 onion, peeled, finely chopped
3x15ml/3tbs/4tbs salad oil
2x15ml/2tbs/3tbs white wine
vinegar
2x15ml/2tbs/3tbs double cream
(heavy cream)
1x5ml/1tsp/1tsp grated
horseradish - from a jar
1x5ml/1tsp/1tsp castor sugar
(fine granulated)
salt and pepper

Garnish
chives, finely chopped

Method

Wash the spinach thoroughly and leave to drain. Shake dry.
Remove the stems from the tomatoes and cut into 8 pieces. Slice
the eggs.
Mix the onion with the oil, vinegar, cream, horseradish and sugar.
Season. Put the salad into a bowl, pour over the dressing. Garnish
with chives.

Spinach salad

Mushroom, radish, endive medley

Ingredients

For the salad
225g/8oz/½ lb mushrooms

For the marinade
3x15ml/3tbs/4tbs wine vinegar
1x15ml/1tbs/2tbs salad oil
salt and pepper
castor sugar (fine granulated)
1 bunch radishes
100g/4oz/ ¼ lb endive

For the dressing
250ml/8fl oz/1 cup soured cream
1x15ml/1tbs/2tbs tomato
ketchup (catsup)
1x15ml/1tbs/2tbs milk
salt and pepper
castor sugar (fine granulated)
4x15ml/4tbs/5tbs mixed herbs,
chopped (parsley, basil, chives)
watercress, chopped

Method

Prepare, wash and slice the mushrooms.
Stir together the vinegar and salad oil. Season with salt, pepper and sugar, mix with mushrooms and leave standing for a white. Trim, rinse and dry the endive, separate the leaves and tear up the largest ones.
Stir together the soured cream, ketchup and milk. Season with salt, pepper and sugar. Add the herbs and cress. Put the radishes, endive and mushrooms into a bowl, pour the dressing over the top and serve at once.

Iceberg salad with bacon

Ingredients

For the salad
1 iceberg lettuce, trimmed,
rinsed, dried
1 onion, peeled
100g/4oz/¼ lb streaky bacon,
de-rinded

For the dressing
2x15ml/2tbs/3tbs salad oil
6x15ml/6tbs/8tbs soured cream
2x15ml/2tbs/3tbs lemon juice
salt and pepper
paprika
2x15ml/2tbs/3tbs parsley,
chopped

Method

Cut the lettuce into 8 sections. Chop the onion and streaky bacon.
Heat a little butter and fry the onion and bacon. Sprinkle the onion
and bacon over the iceberg lettuce. Mix together the oil, soured
cream and lemon juice. Season with salt, pepper and paprika. Stir
in the parsley. Pour the dressing over the salad and serve at once.
Tip: Serve this salad as a light summer meal with brown bread.

Iceberg salad with bacon

Chinese cabbage with cream dressing

Ingredients

For the salad
500g/1lb/1lb Chinese cabbage

For the dressing
25g/2oz/4tbs cottage cheese
3x15ml/3tbs/4tbs double cream
(heavy cream)
3x15ml/3tbs/4tbs soured cream

2x15ml/2tbs/3tbs wine vinegar
salt and pepper
castor sugar (fine granulated)
1x15ml/1tbs/2tbs parsley,
chopped
1x15ml/1tbs/2tbs chives,
snipped

Method

Discard the outermost leaves of the cabbage. Cut in half and slice the leaves into narrow strips. Rinse and leave to drain. Mix the cottage cheese, cream, soured cream and vinegar. Season with salt, pepper and sugar. Stir in the parsley and chives. Mix the dressing with the cabbage, check seasoning. Serve at once.

Lamb's lettuce or endive salad Düsseldorf

Ingredients

For the salad
175g/6oz/6oz lamb's lettuce or
endive
2 medium-sized oranges, peeled
1 bunch spring onions,
trimmed, washed

For the dressing
4x15ml/4tbs/5tbs soured cream
1x15ml/1tbs/2tbs salad oil
3x15ml/3tbs/4tbs lemon juice
salt and pepper
castor sugar (fine granulated)
ground ginger

Method
Trim and rinse the lamb's lettuce or endive, tear up the larger leaves. Remove the white pith from the oranges, cut into sections then cut in half. Slice the spring onions.
Stir together the soured cream, oil and lemon juice. Season with salt, pepper, sugar and ground ginger. Pour the dressing over.

Piquant salad

Ingredients

For the salad
225g/8oz/½ lb lamb's lettuce
or endive
2 hardboiled eggs, shelled

For the dressing
½ clove garlic, peeled

1 small onion, peeled
3x15ml/3tbs/4tbs salad oil
1x15ml/1tbs/2tbs white wine
vinegar
salt and pepper
3x15ml/3tbs/4tbs chives, finely
chopped

Method
Trim and rinse the lamb's lettuce or endive, tear up the larger leaves.
Quarter the eggs and put with the lettuce or endive in bowls.
Crush the garlic, finely chop the onion. Stir into the oil and
vinegar. Season and add the chives. Pour the dressing over the
salad and serve at once.

Lamb's lettuce or endive salad Düsseldorf   *Piquant salad*

Iceberg salad with mango

Ingredients

For the salad
1 small iceberg lettuce,
trimmed, rinsed, dried,
torn into pieces
1 ripe mango
100g/4oz/¼ lb boiled ham,
sliced
2 hardboiled eggs, shelled
6 radishes

For the dressing
2x15ml/2tbs/3tbs mixed herbs,
chopped (parsley, tarragon,
chives)
150ml/¼ pt/⅔ cup soured
cream
120ml/4fl oz/½ cup milk
1x15ml/1tbs/2tbs tomato
ketchup (catsup)
lemon juice
salt
freshly ground white pepper
paprika
castor sugar (fine granulated)

Method

Peel the mango, remove the pip and cut the fruit into small pieces.
Dice the ham. Prepare and wash the radishes. Slice the eggs and
radishes and put all the salad ingredients into a bowl. Stir together
the soured cream, milk and tomato ketchup. Season with lemon
juice, salt, pepper, paprika and sugar. Stir in the herbs. Pour the
dressing over the salad and serve at once.

Iceberg lettuce salad Thessa

(4-6 portions)

Ingredients

For the salad
1 iceberg lettuce, trimmed,
rinsed, dried, torn into pieces
2 oranges, peeled

1 apple, peeled, cored
lemon juice
150g/5oz/5oz white grapes

For the dressing
4x15ml/4tbs/5tbs double cream
(heavy cream)
2x15ml/2tbs/3tbs lemon juice
salt

freshly ground white pepper
sugar
3x15ml/3tbs/4tbs mustard and
cress

Method

Remove the pith and skin from the oranges. Quarter the apple.
Cut the fruit into pieces. Sprinkle the apple with lemon juice.
Wash the grapes, halve and remove the pips. Put the salad
ingredients into a bowl or individual bowls.
Stir the lemon juice into the cream. Season with salt, freshly
ground white pepper and sugar. Pour the dressing over the salad.
Sprinkle the salad with cress, serve at once.

Iceberg lettuce salad Thessa

Fresh vegetable salads

Cucumber tomato salad

(illustrated page 38-39)

Ingredients

For the salad
1 cucumber
375g/12oz/ ¾ lb tomatoes
1 bunch watercress

For the dressing
4x15ml/4tbs/5tbs salad oil
1x15ml/1tbs/2tbs wine vinegar
salt and pepper
castor sugar (fine granulated)
1 hardboiled egg, shelled

Method

Cut the tips from the cucumber, cut in half lengthways then slice thinly. Remove seeds from tomatoes, halve and slice. Rinse watercress and drain. Arrange the ingredients on individual dishes. Stir the vinegar into the oil. Season with salt, pepper and sugar. Pour the dressing over the salad. Remove the yolk from the egg and chop finely. Sprinkle over the salad, together with the finely sliced white.

Tomatoes with black radish sauce

Ingredients

For the salad
225g/8oz/ ½ lb tomatoes
3 hardboiled eggs, shelled

For the dressing
1 large black radish
salt
250ml/8fl oz/1 cup soured cream
2x15ml/2tbs/3tbs chives, finely chopped

Method

Slice the tomatoes and eggs and arrange them on a flat dish, sprinkle with salt. Prepare, grate and wash the radish, sprinkle with salt and leave until the salt is absorbed. Mix the radish with the soured cream and chives. Season with salt and pour on to the tomato and egg.

Gourmet salad with kiwifruit dressing

Ingredients

For the salad
1 fennel bulb
1 red pepper, halved
2 courgettes (zucchini)
3 spring onions
4 kiwifruit, peeled

For the dressing
2 kiwifruit, peeled
1x15ml/1tbs/2tbs walnut oil
1x15ml/1tbs/2tbs lemon juice
2x15ml/2tbs/3tbs dry sherry
1x5ml/1tsp/1tsp honey
pinch cayenne pepper
1 egg yolk
4x15ml/4tbs/5tbs soured cream
salt
fennel leaves

Method

Finely chop the fennel leaves and reserve. Divide the fennel into quarters and slice finely. Remove the stalk, seeds and ribs of the pepper, wash and slice. Cut the tips off the courgettes, cut into thin slices. Wash and trim the spring onions, then slice thinly. Slice the kiwifruit.
Coarsely chop the remaining 2 kiwifruit and rub through a sieve. Mix with the walnut oil, lemon juice, dry sherry, honey, cayenne pepper. Mix the egg yolk with soured cream and stir into the dressing. Season with salt. Mix the dressing with the salad.
Sprinkle the chopped fennel leaves over the salad. Serve at once.

Kohlrabi salad

Ingredients

For the salad
500g/1lb/1lb kohlrabi

For the dressing
3x15ml/3tbs/4tbs lemon juice
6x15ml/6tbs/8tbs soured cream

salt
castor sugar (fine granulated)
washed lettuce leaves
1x15ml/1tbs/2tbs parsley,
chopped

Method

Peel, wash and grate the kohlrabi.
Stir the soured cream into the lemon juice. Season with salt and sugar. Mix the kohlrabi with the dressing. Put the salad on the lettuce and sprinkle with parsley.

Spring symphony

(facing page)

Ingredients

For the salad
1 lettuce, washed, trimmed,
leaves separated, dried
1 small fennel bulb
1 bunch radishes
½ red pepper
½ green pepper
1 avocado

For the dressing
5x15ml/5tbs/6tbs salad oil
2x15ml/2tbs/3tbs wine vinegar
salt and pepper
castor sugar (fine granulated)
chives, finely chopped

Method

Prepare, wash and quarter the fennel and radishes. Slice thinly. Remove stems, seeds and ribs from the peppers. Cut across in thin strips. Cut the avocado lengthways. Remove the stone, peel and slice. Put the salad into a bowl.
Stir the vinegar into the oil. Season with salt, pepper and sugar. Stir in the chives. Pour over the salad and toss well.

Summer watercress salad

Ingredients

For the salad
100g/4oz/¼ lb watercress
1 bunch radishes
4 tomatoes
salt and pepper

For the dressing
3x15ml/3tbs/4tbs salad oil
1x15ml/1tbs/2tbs wine vinegar
1x5ml/1tsp/1tsp mustard
castor sugar (fine granulated)
Garnish
2 hardboiled eggs (optional)

Method

Rinse and dry the watercress. Arrange on a flat serving dish.
Prepare and wash the radishes, slice. Thinly slice the tomatoes.
Arrange in a circle on top of the cress. Sprinkle with salt and
pepper, place the radish slices on top.
Stir together the salad oil, vinegar and mustard. Season to taste
with sugar and pour over the salad. Shell and chop the eggs and
sprinkle over the salad.

Salad potpourri

(facing page)

Ingredients

For the salad
3 small onions, peeled, sliced
50g/2oz/4tbs button
mushrooms
1 bunch radishes
1 red apple, peeled, cored
2 hardboiled eggs, shelled
175g/6oz/6oz tinned tangerines
1 lettuce, trimmed, washed,
dried

For the dressing
4x15ml/4tbs/5tbs olive oil
2x15ml/2tbs/3tbs lemon juice
salt and pepper
castor sugar (fine granulated)
3x15ml/3tbs/4tbs herbs,
chopped (chervil, tarragon)

Method
Wash the mushrooms and radishes. Cut these and the onions into

thin slices. Quarter the apple and slice. Finely chop the hardboiled eggs. Drain the tangerines.

Stir the lemon juice into the oil and season with salt, pepper and sugar. Stir in the herbs. Separate the lettuce leaves, tear the larger ones into pieces. Mix the dressing with the salad, toss well and serve immediately.

Spicy red cabbage salad

Ingredients

For the salad
1 small red cabbage
1 medium-sized onion, peeled

For the dressing
1x15ml/1tbs/2tbs treacle
3x15ml/3tbs/4tbs red wine vinegar
1x15ml/1tbs/2tbs mustard
salt and pepper

Method

Discard the outermost leaves from the cabbage. Cut into 4 pieces, remove the stalk. Wash and drain well, shred finely. Thinly slice the onion.
Stir together the treacle, vinegar and mustard. Season. Mix the dressing with the salad and serve immediately.

Seville style tomatoes

(8 portions)

Ingredients

For the salad
500g/1lb/1lb tomatoes, halved
salt
2 onions, peeled
1 bunch spring onions

For the dressing
4x15ml/4tbs/5tbs salad oil
1x15ml/1tbs/2tbs wine vinegar
4 small red peppers

Method

Stir the vinegar into the oil. Remove the stems from the peppers and cut in half lengthways. Remove the seeds and ribs, cut the peppers into small pieces, add them to the oil and vinegar.
Leave to soak for about 12 hours.

Remove the seeds and stems from the tomatoes. Dice, season with salt. Finely chop the onion. Wash and trim the spring onions, slice finely. Mix the salad with the pepper dressing. Chill for 10 minutes.

Spicy persimmon salad

Ingredients

For the salad
4 firm persimmons
1 large apple, peeled, cored
lemon juice
1 medium-sized onion, peeled
washed lettuce leaves

For the dressing
2x15ml/2tbs/3tbs salad oil
1x15ml/1tbs/2tbs wine vinegar
4x15ml/4tbs/5tbs soy sauce
castor sugar (fine granulated)

Method

Remove the leaves from the persimmons, halve and slice thinly.
Quarter the apple, cut into slices. Sprinkle with lemon juice.
Slice the onion into thin rings. Cover 4 bowls with lettuce and
arrange the salad ingredients on top.
Stir together the salad oil, vinegar and soy sauce. Add sugar to
taste. Pour the dressing over the salad ingredients.

Spicy persimmon salad

Fennel salad

Ingredients

For the salad
3 small fennel bulbs

For the dressing
4x15ml/4tbs/5tbs salad oil
2x15ml/2tbs/3tbs lemon juice
salt
sugar

Method

Prepare and wash the fennel, cut into narrow slices.
Stir the lemon juice into the oil. Season. Mix the dressing with the
fennel. Add additional salt, sugar and lemon juice to taste.

"Nouvelle cuisine" salad

(2 portions)

Ingredients

For the salad
10 dried morels
4 tomatoes, blanched, skinned,
peeled
½ head curly lettuce (batavia)
100g/4oz/4oz endive
1 hardboiled egg, shelled
½ clove garlic, peeled

For the dressing
1x15ml/1tbs/2tbs morel liquid
2x15ml/2tbs/3tbs olive oil
1x15ml/1tbs/2tbs wine vinegar
2x15ml/2tbs/3tbs medium
sherry
salt
castor sugar (fine granulated)
1x2.5ml/½ tsp/½ tsp preserved
green peppercorns

Method

Rinse the morels thoroughly under cold running water. Fill the pan
with enough water to generously cover the morels and leave to soak
for 2 hours. Bring the water to the boil and cook for 10 minutes.
Remove and leave to drain and cool. Pour the cooking liquid
through filter paper and reduce it to approx 1x15ml/1tbs/2tbs. Slice

the tomatoes. Wash and dry the lettuce, separate the leaves. Wash and prepare the endive, tear the larger leaves. Cut the egg into quarters. Rub the garlic around the plates. Put the salad ingredients on to the plates.

Stir together the liquid from the morels, the oil, vinegar and sherry. Season with salt and sugar. Crush the peppercorns and stir into the dressing, pour over the salad.

"Nouvelle cuisine" salad

Spring turnip and carrot salad

Ingredients

For the salad
350g/12oz/³/₅ lb young turnips
275g/10oz/10oz carrots
1x15ml/1tbs/2tbs dill, chopped
1x15ml/1tbs/2tbs chives,
chopped

For the dressing
2x15ml/2tbs/3tbs salad oil
1x15ml/1tbs/2tbs herb vinegar
salt and pepper

Method

Prepare and scrape the turnips and carrots, then wash and grate coarsely. Mix with the dill and chives.
Stir the vinegar into the oil. Season. Mix the dressing with the vegetables. Check seasoning and serve chilled.

Andalusian salad

Ingredients

For the salad
1 lettuce
½ cucumber
1 small onion, peeled
3 large tomatoes
50g/2oz/2oz anchovy fillets
5 hardboiled quail's eggs or
2 chicken eggs
20 stuffed olives

For the dressing
6x15ml/6tbs/8tbs olive oil
2x15ml/2tbs/3tbs herb vinegar
salt and pepper
castor sugar (fine granulated)
parsley, chopped

Method

Wash and trim the lettuce, wash and thinly slice the cucumber.
Slice the onions into thin rings. Cut the tomatoes into 8 sections.
Put the anchovies in milk for 10 minutes then drain well. Shell and halve the eggs. Cut the olives in half.
Stir the vinegar into the oil. Season with salt and pepper and sugar.
Mix the dressing with the salad ingredients, sprinkle with parsley.

Refreshing courgettes

Ingredients

For the salad
4 small courgettes (zucchini)
3x15ml/3tbs/4tbs lemon juice
1x15ml/1tbs/2tbs castor sugar
(fine granulated)
washed lettuce leaves

For the dressing
50g/2oz/4tbs cottage cheese,
6x15ml/6tbs/8tbs double cream
(heavy cream)
paprika

Method

Cut the tips off the courgettes, wash, peel and cut into thin slices.
Stir together the lemon juice and sugar and mix with the courgettes.
Put in a cold place.
Arrange the lettuce leaves on a dish and put the courgettes on top.
Mix the cottage cheese with the cream and pour over the salad.
Sprinkle with paprika.

Andalusian salad

Black radish spiral

(1 portion)
Ingredients

1 black radish
salt
washed lettuce leaves
sections of tomato
parsley, chopped

Method

Prepare and peel the radish. Wash and dry then cut with a potato peeler into a spiral shape. Sprinkle with salt and leave until the salt is absorbed.
Place the spiral on lettuce leaves and garnish with sections of tomato and sprinkle with parsley.

Spring salad with egg

(facing page - 2 portions)

Ingredients

For the salad
1 small black radish
½ cucumber
2 tomatoes
washed lettuce leaves

For the dressing
4x15ml/4tbs/5tbs soured cream
1x5ml/1tsp/1tsp sweet mustard
1x15ml/1tbs/2tbs medium sherry
salt and pepper
1 hardboiled egg, shelled
chives, finely chopped

Method
Prepare, peel and wash the black radish. Wash the cucumber and tomatoes. Thinly slice all three ingredients. Line 2 cocktail glasses or bowls with lettuce leaves. Arrange the salad ingredients on top. Stir together the soured cream, mustard and sherry. Season.
Pour the dressing over the salad. Quarter the egg and divide between the dishes. Sprinkle with chives.

Carrot salad with walnuts

Ingredients

For the salad
750g/1¾ lb/1¾ lb carrots
washed lettuce leaves

Garnish
lemon slices

For the dressing
4x15ml/4tbs/5tbs lemon juice
4x15ml/4tbs/5tbs walnut oil
2x15ml/2tbs/3tbs castor sugar
(fine granulated)
salt and pepper
50g/2oz/4tbs walnuts

Method

Scrape and wash the carrots, grate finely.
Stir the sugar and walnut oil into the lemon juice, season. Mix the dressing with the carrots. Chop the walnuts coarsley and mix into the carrots. Leave the salad to stand for about 15 minutes.
Put each portion of the salad on a plate covered with lettuce leaves and garnish with lemon slices.

Colourful vitamin salad

Ingredients

For the salad
400g/14oz/14oz red and yellow
peppers, halved, seeded, cored
1 medium-sized onion, peeled
2 medium-sized oranges, peeled
4 kiwifruit, peeled
1 large apple
lemon juice

For the dressing
3x15ml/3tbs/4tbs salad oil
3x15ml/3tbs/4tbs sherry or
wine vinegar
3x15ml/3tbs/4tbs soy sauce
pepper
castor sugar (fine granulated)

Method

Cut the peppers into thin strips. Cut the onion into slices then
divide into rings. Remove white pith from oranges, halve and cut
into slices. Halve the kiwifruit lengthways and slice. Peel and core
the apple and cut into slices, sprinkle with lemon juice.
Mix the soy sauce and vinegar into the oil. Season with sugar and
pepper. Pour the dressing over the salad ingredients and chill.
Tip: Serve this salad with brown bread and butter as a light supper.

Colourful vitamin salad

Radish salad

Ingredients

For the salad
3 bunches radishes
5 spring onions
1 apple, peeled, cored

For the dressing
3x15ml/3tbs/4tbs salad oil
1x15ml/1tbs/2tbs herb vinegar
salt and pepper
castor sugar (fine granulated)
1x15ml/1tbs/2tbs chives, finely chopped

Method

Wash the radishes and cut into slices. Prepare the onions, cut off leaves to approx 15 cm/6" of onion. Wash onions and cut into rings. Cut the apple into slices.
Stir the vinegar into the oil. Season with salt and pepper and sugar. Stir in the chives. Mix the dressing with salad ingredients. Serve chilled.

Avocados with caper dressing

Ingredients

For the salad
100g/4oz/ ¼ lb radicchio
(Italian red lettuce)
½ head curly lettuce (batavia)
3 avocados

For the dressing
2 spring onions
1 clove garlic, peeled, crushed
1x15ml/1tbs/2tbs capers,
chopped
4x15ml/4tbs/5tbs salad oil
4x15ml/4tbs/5tbs sherry or
wine vinegar
1x15ml/1tbs/2tbs water
salt and pepper
castor sugar (fine granulated)
2x15ml/2tbs/3tbs watercress,
chopped

Method

Rinse and dry the radicchio and batavia, and arrange on individual plates. Halve the avocados lengthways, remove the stone. Peel and cut across in thin slices.

Prepare the spring onions, cut off leaves to give approx 15 cm/6''
of onion, slice finely. Mix onions, garlic and capers with the oil,
vinegar and water. Season with salt and pepper and sugar. Stir in
the watercress. Mix carefully with the avocado slices and arrange
on top of the lettuce leaves.

Avocados with caper dressing

Aperitive salad

Ingredients

For the salad
4 sticks celery
175g/6oz/6oz carrots
2 apples, peeled, cored
lemon juice

For the dressing
150ml/¼pt/⅔ cup yoghurt
3x15ml/3tbs/5tbs soured cream
2x15ml/2tbs/3tbs lemon juice
1x5ml/1tsp/1tsp honey
1x2.5ml/½ tsp/½ tsp mustard
salt and pepper
100g/4oz/¼ lb boiled ham
3x15ml/3tbs/4tbs almonds
blanched, chopped

Method

Remove any tough fibres from celery. Wash and drain, cut into thin slices. Grate carrots coarsely. Cut apples into slices. Sprinkle with lemon juice. Put the salad ingredients into glass bowls or individual plates.
Stir the mustard, honey, lemon juice and soured cream into the yoghurt. Season. Dice the ham and stir into the dressing together with almonds. Pour over the salad.
Garnish with watercress.

Tomato salad

Ingredients

For the salad
750g/1¾ lb/1¾ lb tomatoes

For the dressing
1-2 onions, peeled, finely
chopped
5x15ml/5tbs/6tbs salad oil
2x15ml/2tbs/3tbs wine vinegar

salt and pepper
sugar
2x15ml/2tbs/3tbs chives, finely
chopped

Method

Wash and dry the tomatoes, slice thinly. Mix the onion with the oil and vinegar. Season with salt, pepper and sugar. Stir in the chives. Pour the dressing over the tomato slices.

Cucumber salad with black radish

Ingredients

For the salad
2 black radishes
(approx 500g/1lb/1lb)
1 cucumber
(approx 500g/1lb/1lb)
250g/9oz/9oz sliced roast beef
2x15ml/2tbs/3tbs dill, chopped

For the dressing
5x15ml/5tbs/6tbs salad oil
5x15ml/5tbs/6tbs lemon juice
1x5ml/1tsp/1tsp grated lemon
rind
1x5ml/1tsp/1tsp crushed green
peppercorns
salt and pepper

Method

Peel and wash the radishes. Wash the cucumber, cut off the tops, halve and remove the pips. Coarsley grate the cucumber and black radishes. Cut the roast beef into strips.
Stir the peppercorns, lemon rind and juice into the oil. Season with salt and pepper. Mix with the salad ingredients and chill for about 20 minutes. Stir the dill into the salad. If necessary season to taste.

Savoury fennel salad

Ingredients

For the salad
2 fennel bulbs
3 oranges or 4 tangerines
150g/5oz/5oz boiled ham

For the dressing
150ml/¼ pt/⅔ cup yoghurt
2x15ml/2tbs/3tbs soured cream
1x15ml/1tbs/2tbs white wine
vinegar
salt and pepper
castor sugar (fine granulated)

Method

Prepare and wash the fennel. Cut into thin slices. Peel the oranges or tangerines, remove the white pith and cut into slices. Cut the ham into strips.
Stir the vinegar and soured cream into the yoghurt. Season with salt, pepper and sugar. Mix the dressing with the salad ingredients and serve chilled.

Savoury fennel salad

Delicious fruit salads

Berry dish

(illustrated page 62/63)

Ingredients

175g/6oz/6oz bilberries
175g/6oz/6oz redcurrants
175g/6oz/6oz blackberries
175g/6oz/6oz strawberries
75g/3oz/6tbs icing sugar (confectioners sugar)
2x15ml/2tbs/3tbs Grand Marnier
2x15ml/2tbs/3tbs lemon juice
vanilla icecream (optional)

Method

Pick over the fruit, wash and leave to drain. String the redcurrants and hull the strawberries. Mix the fruit carefully with the sifted icing sugar. Stir in lemon juice and Grand Marnier. Cover the fruit and leave for 1 hour. Put the fruit salad into dessert bowls. Serve with icecream.

Fine fruit salad

Ingredients

1 avocado, halved, stoned, peeled
1 pear, peeled, cored, sliced
lemon juice
1 orange, peeled
250g/9oz/9oz black grapes
150g/5oz/5oz pineapple
2x15ml/2tbs/3tbs castor sugar (fine granulated)
2x15ml/2tbs/3tbs Grand Marnier

Method

Dice the avocado. Cut the pear into slices. Sprinkle both these ingredients with lemon juice. Remove the white pith from the orange, halve and cut into slices. Cut the grapes in half and remove the pips. Cut the pineapple into pieces.

Mix all the ingredients with the sugar and Grand Marnier. Put the fruit salad into a glass bowl, cover and chill for 1 hour.

Serve with whipped cream.

Special melon fruit salad

(6 portions)

Ingredients

1 honeydew melon
4x15ml/4tbs/5tbs raspberry brandy or Framboise
1x15ml/1tbs/2tbs lemon juice
castor sugar (fine granulated)
2 pears
275g/10oz/10oz raspberries
350g/12oz/³⁄₄ lb pineapple (1 large pineapple)
2x15ml/2tbs/3tbs cranberries (from a jar)
4x15ml/4tbs/5tbs white wine

Method

Cut melon in half and remove the pips. Dice the flesh - reserve the empty halves. Stir together the sugar, lemon juice and raspberry brandy or Framboise. Pour it over the fruit and leave to macerate.

Peel and halve the pears. Remove pips and cores, and cut into dice. Pick over the raspberries and hull them.

Peel the pineapple and cut into pieces. Drain the cranberries. Mix the pears, raspberries, pineapple and cranberries with the melon fruit. Add sugar to taste.

Pour the white wine over the salad.

Use a sharp knife and cut the edges of the melon halves into a serrated pattern. Put the fruit salad into the melon halves and chill well.

Fruit salad with liqueur sauce

Ingredients

For the salad
2 bananas, peeled, sliced
2 apples, peeled, cored, sliced
100g/4oz/¼ lb white or black
grapes
2 oranges, peeled
4 apricots, washed, stoned
2x15ml/2tbs/3tbs castor sugar
(fine granulated)

For the sauce
150ml/¼ pt/⅔ cup soured
cream
3x15ml/3tbs/4tbs Grand
Marnier
25g/1oz/2tbs shelled hazelnuts

Method
Sprinkle apple and banana with lemon juice. Wash and drain the
grapes, halve and remove the pips. Remove the pith from the
oranges and divide into segments. Cut the apricots into sections.
Mix all the ingredients with the sugar and put into a glass bowl.
Stir the Grand Marnier into the soured cream. Cut the hazelnuts
into slices and stir into the cream. Pour the sauce over the fruit.

Strawberry dessert

(facing page)

Ingredients

500g/1lb/1lb strawberries
3x15ml/3tbs/4tbs castor sugar (fine granulated)
4x15ml/4tbs/¼ cup wholemeal oat flakes
300ml/½ pt/1 ¼ cups yoghurt

Garnish
wholemeal oat flakes

Method
Hull the strawberries and cut in half. Sprinkle the sugar over the
strawberries and put into individual dessert bowls. Put equal
amounts of oat flakes on each portion of strawberries. Beat chilled
yoghurt and pour over the dessert bowls. Garnish with oat flakes.

Iced grapes

Ingredients

500g/1lb/1lb black and white grapes, washed, drained
3x15ml/3tbs/4tbs castor sugar (fine granulated)
ice cubes
4x15ml/4tbs/5tbs raspberry brandy or Framboise

Method

Cut grapes in half, remove pips and put grapes into a bowl.
Sprinkle the sugar over the fruit. Crush the ice cubes into small
pieces. Half fill 4 champagne glasses with crushed ice. Put the
grapes on top. Pour equal amounts of raspberry brandy or
Framboise into each glass. Serve at once.

Fruit salad Sabra

Ingredients

1 ripe pear
lemon juice
1 mango
175g/6oz/6oz strawberries
225g/8oz/½ lb fresh dates
4x15ml/4tbs/¼ cup white wine
1x15ml/1tbs/2tbs castor sugar (fine granulated)

Method

Peel the pear and quarter, remove pips and core, and cut into
pieces. Sprinkle with lemon juice. Halve the mango, remove stone,
peel and cut into pieces. Hull the strawberries, cut in half. Halve
the dates and remove stones. Take off hard skin and cut the dates
in strips. Stir sugar into white wine. Mix carefully with fruit
ingredients. Chill for an hour before serving.

Apple salad

(2 portions)

Ingredients

2 medium-sized apples
150ml/¼pt/⅔ cup yoghurt
1x15ml/1tbs/2tbs castor sugar (fine granulated)
4x15ml/4tbs/5tbs oat flakes

Method

Quarter the apples, remove the pips and cores, and dice. Mix with the yoghurt and sugar. Stir in the oat flakes.

Variations: Stir in ground hazelnuts, raisins or a little cinnamon.

Fruit salad Sabra

Berry salad with sekt zabaglione

(facing page)

Ingredients

For the salad
225g/8oz/½ lb raspberries
225g/8oz/½ lb redcurrants
1x15ml/1tbs/2tbs castor sugar
(fine granulated)

For the sekt zabaglione
2 egg yolks
1 egg
2x15ml/2tbs/3tbs castor sugar
(fine granulated)
1x15ml/1tbs/2tbs lemon juice
250ml/8fl oz/1 cup medium
dry sekt (German champagne)

Method

Hull the raspberries, string the redcurrants and wash and drain
well. Set aside a few bunches of redcurrants for garnish.
Divide the raspberries and redcurrants into individual dessert bowls.
Sprinkle with sugar, and chill. Put the yolks together with the
whole egg, sugar, lemon juice and half the sekt into a bowl over a
pan of hot water. Whisk until the mixture is creamy and light.
Pour 120ml/4fl oz/ ½ cup sekt over the fruit then pour warm
zabaglione over. Garnish with bunches of redcurrants and serve at
once.

Kiwifruit salad

Ingredients

For the salad
4 kiwifruits, peeled, sliced
350g/12oz/¾ lb strawberries
2 peaches

For the sauce
4x15ml/4tbs/5tbs orange juice
2x15ml/2tbs/3tbs lemon juice
2x15ml/2tbs/3tbs Grand
Marnier
2x15ml/2tbs/3tbs castor sugar
(fine granulated)

Method
Hull the strawberries and quarter. Put the peaches into boiling water (do not boil). Plunge into cold water and peel. Halve and remove the stones, then cut into slices. Stir the Grand Marnier, lemon and orange juice together. Stir in the sugar and heat the liquid in a saucepan until the sugar has dissolved. Leave the mixture to cool a little, then mix the lukewarm sauce with the fruit salad. Leave until cold.

Berries with strawberry cream

Ingredients

For the berry mixture
150g/5oz/5oz bilberries
150g/5oz/5oz redcurrants
150g/5oz/5oz blackberries
150g/5oz/5oz raspberries
2x15ml/2tbs/3tbs castor sugar
(fine granulated)

For the sauce
150g/5oz/5oz strawberries
1x5ml/1tsp/1tsp vanilla essence
(extract)
250ml/8fl oz/1 cup cream
1x15ml/1tbs/2tbs raspberry
brandy or Framboise

Method

Pick over the berries, wash and leave to drain. String the
redcurrants, hull the raspberries. Mix the fruit with sugar and put
into glass bowl. Wash strawberries and drain. Hull them and cut
into small pieces. Stir raspberry brandy or Framboise and vanilla
into cream. Lightly whip the cream. Stir in the strawberries and
pour over the berries. Serve at once.

Berry salad

(facing page)

Ingredients

750g/1¾ lb/1¾ lb prepared berries (strawberries, redcurrants,
gooseberries, raspberries, blackberries, bilberries, grapes)
2x15ml/2tbs/3tbs castor sugar (fine granulated)
3x15ml/3tbs/4tbs raspberry brandy of Framboise
250ml/8fl oz/1 cup cream

Method

Mix all the berries with the sugar and the raspberry brandy or
Framboise. Cover the fruit and leave to stand for 1 hour. Divide
the fruit into individual dessert bowls. Beat cream until stiff. Put
into a piping bag with a rose nozzle and pipe decoratively over the
fruit.

Cherry apple salad with yoghurt sauce

Ingredients

For the salad
500g/1lb/1lb sweet cherries
2 sour apples, peeled, cored
3x15ml/3tbs/4tbs castor sugar

For the sauce
120ml/4fl oz/½ cup double
cream (heavy cream)
1x5ml/1tsp/1tsp vanilla essence
(extract)
150ml/¼ pt/⅔ cup yoghurt
2x15ml/2tbs/3tbs lemon juice

Method

Remove stalks and stones from cherries. Quarter and thinly slice
the apples. Combine apples and cherries and mix with sugar. Whip
the cream with vanilla until stiff. Stir the lemon juice into the
yoghurt. Fold into the cream. Put the fruit into a glass bowl or
into individual dessert dishes and pour the sauce over the fruit.

Fruit salad

Ingredients

750g/1¾ lb/1¾ lb prepared fruit (strawberries, bananas, white
grapes, oranges)
50g/2oz/2oz prepared redcurrants
castor sugar (fine granulated)
lemon juice

Method

Cut the fruit into pieces and mix with the redcurrants. Sprinkle with a little sugar and lemon juice. Put into dessert bowls.

Fruit salad

Melon cocktail

Ingredients

1 honeydew melon
175g/6oz/6oz tinned lychees, drained, halved
150g/5oz/5oz black or white grapes
150g/5oz/5oz strawberries
lemon juice
castor sugar (fine granulated)
white rum
mint leaves

Method

Cut the melon in half and remove pips. Make little balls of fruit with a spoon or scoop. Keep the empty melon halves. Wash the grapes and strawberries, and drain well. Cut fruit in half and remove pips from grapes. Mix all the fruit together. Flavour with lemon juice and rum. Put the cocktail into the empty halves of melon. Garnish with mint leaves.

Tip: Flavour cream with vanilla essence or white rum. Beat the cream until stiff, then decorate the melon cocktail.

Morning salad with avocado

Ingredients

For the salad
1 avocado, halved, stoned, peeled
1 large banana, peeled, sliced
lemon juice
2 oranges
150g/5oz/5oz fresh dates,
halved, stoned
100g/4oz/4oz strawberries, washed
1 kiwifruit
50g/2oz/2oz raisins, washed

For the sauce
150ml/¼ pt/⅔ cup yoghurt
2x15ml/2tbs/3tbs buttermilk
2x15ml/2tbs/3tbs lemon juice
1x15ml/1tbs/2tbs castor sugar
(fine granulated)

Method

Cut the avocado across in slices and sprinkle this and the banana
with lemon juice. Peel the oranges, remove white pith and skin on
segments. Cut the dates in strips. Remove the cores from the
strawberries and cut into quarters. Peel the kiwifruit, halve and
slice. Put all the salad ingredients into dessert bowls.
Stir the sugar, lemon juice and buttermilk into the yoghurt.
Pour the sauce over the fruit salad and serve at once.

Morning salad with avocados

Savoury and sweet
salad dressings

Interesting facts about vinegar

Vinegar has been known for more than 5000 years as a souring and flavouring agent, but it has also been known and appreciated as a drink. Wine, brandy, fruit wine and other alcohols are used as the basic ingredients for making vinegar (fermented vinegar).
Vinegar bacteria together with oxygen transform alcohol into vinegar. The manufacturers of vinegar allow this fermenting process to take place in large wooden or high quality steel barrels, so-called vinegar makers. Fresh vinegar must rest in the barrels until it has reached the right degree of maturity. Only then can it be filtered and bottled.
By using different basic ingredients and different flavours the following types of vinegar originate:
Wine vinegar is made purely from wine and has an acidity degree of 6%. It has the specific taste originating from wine and that is why it is counted as a particular speciality in the gourmet kitchen.
Wine-brandy vinegar is made from one quarter pure wine vinegar and three quarters brandy vinegar. Thus this vinegar keeps its refreshing spicy sour taste with an acidity degree of 5%.
Brandy vinegar is made out of agricultural alcohol that is generally obtained from sugarbeets, grain or potatoes. Is has a refreshing sour taste.
Herb vinegar is also a popular kind of vinegar, to which delicate herbs or herb derivatives have been added - herbs such as tarragon, balm and dill, of which the flavour making aromatic substances dissolve in the vinegar solution. This type of vinegar needs to be left for a longer period before bottling in order to develop the full delicately spiced flavour.
Fruit vinegar is usually made out of apple wine and has an acidity degree of 5%. It is particularly suitable for the preparation of a refreshing salad. Fruit vinegar is also recommended by many doctors, e.g. mixed with honey as a health drink to be taken in the morning.
Lemon vinegar is a brandy vinegar to which lemon juice has been added. Sometimes this vinegar has a natural cloudy appearance because of the juice.
With these many types of vinegar, salads, salad dressings and other dishes can be given an individual character as far as taste is concerned.

Cocktail dressing

Ingredients

150ml/¼ lb/²⁄₃ *cup soured cream*
3x15ml/3tbs/4tbs tomato ketchup (catsup)
2x15ml/2tbs/3tbs dry white wine
1x15ml/1tbs/2tbs cognac
1x5ml/1tsp/1tsp bottled horseradish sauce
freshly ground pepper
cayenne pepper
mixed herbs, chopped
salt

Method

Mix the horseradish sauce, cognac, white wine, and tomato ketchup
into the soured cream. Season with salt, pepper and cayenne. Stir
in the herbs.
Serve this dressing with fish and vegetable salads, iceberg lettuce,
all exotic salads or as a dipping sauce with meat fondue.

Egg dressing

Ingredients

2x15ml/2tbs/3tbs salad oil
1x15ml/1tbs/2tbs vinegar
1 raw egg yolk
1x5ml/1tsp/1tsp strong mustard
salt and pepper
dill or parsley, finely chopped

Method

Stir the mustard, egg yolk, and vinegar into the salad oil. Season
with salt and pepper. Stir in the dill or parsley.
Egg dressing is especially good with green, cucumber and vegetable
salads.

Spicy cream dressing

Ingredients

2x15ml/2tbs/3tbs soured cream
1x15ml/1tbs/2tbs yoghurt
1 raw egg yolk
1x5ml/1tsp/1tsp mustard, Dijon
1x15ml/1tbs/2tbs onion, finely chopped
2X15ml/2tbs/3tbs white wine vinegar
salt
ground nutmeg

Method

Stir the vinegar, onion, mustard, egg yolk and yoghurt into the soured cream. Season with salt and ground nutmeg.

This dressing is particularly good with green and vegetable salads.

Vinaigrette

Ingredients

1 small onion, peeled, chopped
2 hardboiled eggs, shelled, chopped
2 cocktail gherkins, diced
a few capers, chopped
3x15ml/3tbs/4tbs salad oil
2x15ml/2tbs/3tbs vinegar
1x5ml/1tsp/1tsp strong mustard
salt and pepper
herbs, chopped (optional)

Method

Stir the mustard and vinegar into the salad oil. Add the remaining ingredients. Season with salt and pepper. If required, stir in the herbs.
Vinaigrette is especially good with green, vegetable, meat and fish salads.

Vinaigrette

Cognac sauce

Ingredients

1x5ml/1tsp/1tsp cornflour (cornstarch)
120ml/4fl oz/½ cup milk
2x15ml/2tbs/3tbs castor sugar (fine granulate)
2 raw egg yolks
2x15ml/2tbs/3tbs cognac

Method

Blend the cornflour with 2x15ml/2tbs/3tbs of the milk. Add sugar.
Bring the rest of the milk to the boil. Take the pan off the heat
and mix in the blended cornflour, stirring constantly. Bring back to
the boil and remove. Whisk the yolks with a little of the hot sauce.
Add the egg mixture to the sauce, stirring constantly. Heat up once
again but do not boil. Stir in cognac.
Serve with apple strudel or stewed pears.

Pesto

(Italian basic dressing)

Ingredients

4 cloves garlic, peeled, crushed
1x5ml/1tsp/1tsp salt
50g/2oz/4tbs pine kernels
8x15ml/8tbs/10tbs basil, chopped
50g/2oz/4tbs Pecorino cheese, grated
50g/2oz/4tbs Parmesan cheese, grated
200ml/⅓ pt/⅛ cup olive oil

Method

Mix garlic together with the salt, pine kernels and basil into a motar and pound with a pestle until it is creamy. Add cheese and mix in with the other ingredients. Stir in the olive oil a little at a time. Serve Pesto with pastas and vegetable soup.

Tip: If no pestle and mortar is available, cream the ingredients (basil, garlic, salt, pine kernels) with an electric mixer, then carry on with the recipe. If Pecorino is unavailable, use double quantity of Parmesan.

Using a pestle and mortar to make pesto

Red wine herb dressing

Ingredients

2 hardboiled eggs
1 raw egg yolk
120ml/4fl oz/½ cup salad oil
3x15ml/3tbs/4tbs vinegar
3x15ml/3tbs/4tbs red wine
1x2.5ml/½ tsp/½ tsp ground white pepper
salt
castor sugar (fine granulated)
1x15ml/1tbs/2tbs tarragon, finely chopped
2x15ml/2tbs/3tbs parsley, finely chopped

Method

Shell the eggs. Chop the whites finely and reserve. Mash the yolks, with the raw egg yolk, salad oil, vinegar, red wine and ground white pepper. Season with salt and sugar. Stir in the chopped egg whites, tarragon and parsley.

Sherry cream dressing

Ingredients

1 raw egg yolk
1x15ml/1tbs/2tbs castor sugar (fine granulated)
2x15ml/2tbs/3tbs dry sherry
1x15ml/1tbs/2tbs lemon juice
2x15ml/2tbs/3tbs whipped cream
1x15ml/1tbs/2tbs toasted almonds, blanched, chopped

Method

Stir the egg yolk with the sugar until the mixture is frothy. Add the sherry and lemon juice. Fold in the whipped cream. Just before serving, sprinkle the almonds over the dressing.
Serve with fruit salad or an ice-cream dessert.

Herb dressing

Ingredients

150ml/½ pt/⅔ cup soured cream
3x15ml/3tbs/4tbs tomato ketchup (catsup)
salt and pepper
castor sugar (fine granulated)
paprika
2x15ml/2tbs/3tbs mixed herbs, chopped

Method

Stir the tomato ketchup through the soured cream. Season with salt, pepper, sugar and paprika. Stir in the herbs.

Herb dressing

Salad dressing

Ingredients

1 medium-sized onion, peeled, finely chopped
2x15ml/2tbs/3tbs double cream (heavy)
3x15ml/3tbs/4tbs salad oil
2x15ml/2tbs/3tbs lemon juice or vinegar
salt, castor sugar (fine granulated)
1x15ml/1tbs/2tbs mixed herbs, chopped

Method

Mix onion with the cream, salad oil, and lemon juice or vinegar.
Season with salt and sugar. Stir in the herbs.

Lemon balm dressing

Ingredients

200ml/⅓ pt/⅛ cup yoghurt
3x15ml/3tbs/4tbs lemon juice
sugar
2x15ml/2tbs/3tbs lemon balm leaves, finely chopped
lemon balm leaves for garnish

Method

Stir the sugar and lemon juice into the yoghurt. Stir in the chopped
lemon balm leaves. Sprinkle the whole lemon balm leaves over the
top of the dressing to garnish.

Use this dressing with lettuce.

Pomegranate sauce

Ingredients

2 pomegranates
1x15ml/1tbs/2tbs grenadine syrup
1x15ml/1tbs/2tbs lemon juice
2x15ml/2tbs/3tbs Grand Marnier or white rum
1x15ml/1tbs/2tbs icing sugar (confectioners sugar), sifted
120ml/4fl oz/½ cup dry white wine

Method

Cut the pomegranates in quarters. Take out the fruit and the pips.
Mix together with grenadine syrup, lemon juice, Grand Marnier or
white rum and icing sugar. Stir in the dry white wine.
Serve this sauce with fruit salad made from exotic fruits.

Pomegranate sauce

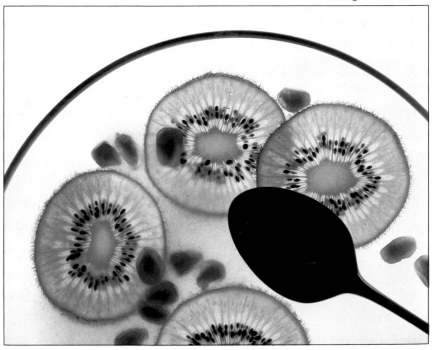

Contents

Foreword 4
California salad 6
Chicory salad with horseradish 7
Crispy leaf salads 8
Spinach salad with oranges 10
Radicchio with lamb's lettuce 10
Savoury Chinese cabbage salad 11
Watercress salad 12
Iceberg salad 12
Iceberg salad with kiwifruit 14
Nut and apple salad 14
Spanish salad 16
Radicchio asparagus salad 16
Bulgarian endive salad 18
Endive apple salad 18
Basic lettuce salad 19
Salad with walnut dressing 20
Summer salad 20
Iceberg salad Gisela 22
Sweetcorn salad 22
Chicory salad with cheese dressing 24
Iceberg salad with fruit 24
Winter salad 26
Salad with cream cheese dressing 26
Endive and mushroom salad 28
Spanish endive and pepper salad 28
Chinese cabbage salad 30
Spinach salad 30
Mushroom, radish, endive medley 32
Iceberg salad with bacon 32
Chinese cabbage with cream dressing 34
Lamb's lettuce or endive salad Düsseldorf 34
Piquant salad 35
Iceberg salad with mango 36
Iceberg lettuce salad Thessa 36
Fresh vegetable salads 38
Cucumber tomato salad 40
Tomatoes with black radish sauce 40
Gourmet salad with kiwifruit dressing 41
Kohlrabi salad 42
Spring symphony 42
Summer watercress salad 44
Salad potpourri 44
Spicy red cabbage salad 46
Seville style tomatoes 46
Spicy persimmon salad 47
Fennel salad 48

"Nouvelle cuisine" salad 48
Spring turnip and carrot salad 50
Andalusian salad 50
Refreshing courgettes 51
Black radish spiral 52
Spring salad with egg 52
Carrot salad with walnuts 54
Colourful vitamin salad 54
Radish salad 56
Avocados with caper dressing 56
Aperitive salad 58
Tomato salad 60
Cucumber salad with black radish 60
Savoury fennel salad 61
Delicious fruit salads 62
Berry dish 64
Fine fruit salad 64
Special melon fruit salad 65
Fruit salad with liqueur sauce 66
Strawberry dessert 66
Iced grapes 68
Fruit salad Sabra 68
Apple salad 69
Berry salad with sekt zabaglione 70
Kiwifruit salad 70
Berries with strawberry cream 72
Berry salad 72
Cherry apple salad with yoghurt sauce 74
Fruit salad 74
Melon cocktail 76
Morning salad with avocado 76
Savoury and sweet dressings 78
Interesting facts about vinegar 80
Cocktail dressing 81
Egg dressing 81
Spicy cream dressing 82
Vinaigrette 82
Cognac sauce 84
Pesto 84
Red wine herb dressing 86
Sherry cream dressing 86
Herb dressing 87
Salad dressing 88
Lemon balm dressing 88
Pomegranate sauce 89

Index

Apple
Chicory salad with
horseradish, 7
Nut and apple salad, 14
Endive apple salad, 18
Iceberg salad Gisela, 22
Iceberg lettuce salad
Thessa, 36
Salad potpourri, 44
Spicy persimmon salad, 47
Colourful vitamin salad, 54
Aperitive salad, 58
Fruit salad with liqueur
sauce, 66
Apple salad, 69
Cherry apple salad with
yoghurt sauce, 74

Avocado
Spring symphony, 42
Avocados with caper
dressing, 56
Fine fruit salad, 64
Morning salad with
avocado, 76

Cabbage
Savoury Chinese cabbage
salad, 11
Chinese cabbage salad, 30
Spicy red cabbage salad, 46

Cheese
Bulgarian endive salad, 18
Summer salad, 20
Chicory salad with cheese
dressing, 24
Salad with cream cheese
dressing, 26
Chinese cabbage with cream
dressing, 34
Refreshing courgettes, 51
Pesto, 84

Chicory
Chicory salad with
horseradish, 7

Chicory salad with cheese
dressing, 24
Cream
California salad, 6
Chicory salad with
horseradish, 7
Bulgarian endive salad, 18
Summer salad, 20
Salad with cream cheese
dressing, 26
Endive and mushroom salad, 28
Spinach salad, 30
Chinese cabbage salad, 30
Mushroom, radish, endive
medley, 32
Iceberg salad with bacon, 32
Lamb's lettuce or endive salad
Düsseldorf, 34
Iceberg salad with mango, 36
Iceberg lettuce salad
Thessa, 36
Tomatoes with black radish
sauce, 40
Gourmet salad with kiwifruit
dressing, 41
Kohlrabi salad, 42
Refreshing courgettes, 51
Spring salad with egg, 52
Aperitive salad, 58
Savoury fennel salad, 61
Fruit salad with liqueur
sauce, 66
Berries with strawberry
cream, 72
Berry salad, 72
Cherry apple salad with
yoghurt sauce, 74
Cocktail dressing, 81
Spicy cream dressing, 82
Pesto, 84
Sherry cream dressing, 86
Herb dressing, 87
Salad dressing, 88

Cucumber
Spanish salad, 16

Summer salad, 20
Cucumber tomato salad, 40
Andalusian salad, 50
Spring salad with egg, 52
Cucumber salad with black
    radish, 60

Egg
    Radicchio with lamb's lettuce, 10
    Watercress salad, 12
    Spanish salad, 16
    Sweetcorn salad, 22
    Iceberg salad Gisela, 22
    Spanish endive and pepper salad, 28
    Spinach salad, 30
    Piquant salad, 35
    Iceberg salad with mango, 36
    Cucumber tomato salad, 40
    Tomato with black radish sauce, 40
    Gourmet salad with kiwifruit dressing, 41
    Salad potpourri, 44
    "Nouvelle cuisine" salad, 48
    Spring salad with egg, 52
    Berry salad with sekt zabaglione, 70
    Egg dressing, 81
    Spicy cream dressing, 82
    Cognac sauce, 84
    Red wine herb dressing, 86
    Sherry cream dressing, 86

Endive
    Endive apple salad, 18
    Bulgarian endive salad, 18
    Winter salad, 26
    Spanish endive and pepper
        salad, 28
    Endive and mushroom salad, 28
    Mushroom, radish, endive
        medley, 32
    Lamb's lettuce or endive
        salad Düsseldorf, 34
    Piquant salad, 35
    "Nouvelle cuisine" salad, 48

Fennel
    Gourmet salad with kiwifruit dres-
        sing, 41
    Spring symphony, 42
    Fennel salad, 48
    Savoury fennel salad, 61

Iceberg lettuce
    California salad, 6
    Iceberg salad, 12
    Iceberg salad with kiwifruit, 14
    Iceberg salad Gisela, 22
    Iceberg salad with fruit, 24
    Iceberg salad with bacon, 32
    Iceberg lettuce salad Thessa, 36
    Iceberg salad with mango, 36

Kiwifruit
    Iceberg salad with kiwifruit, 14
    Gourmet salad with kiwifruit
        dressing, 41
    Colourful vitamin salad, 54
    Kiwifruit salad, 70

Lemon balm dressing, 88

Lettuce
    Radicchio with lamb's lettuce salad, 10
    Radicchio asparagus salad, 16
    Basic lettuce salad, 19
    Sweetcorn salad, 22
    Lamb's lettuce or endive salad
        Düsseldorf, 34

Melon
    California salad, 6
    Special melon fruit salad, 65
    Melon cocktail, 76

Mushroom
    Radicchio asparagus salad, 16
    Iceberg salad Gisela, 22
    Endive and mushroom salad, 28
    Mushroom, radish, endive
        medley, 32
    Salad potpourri, 44

Nuts
    California salad, 6
    Iceberg salad with kiwifruit, 14
    Nut salad, 14
    Salad with walnut dressing, 20
    Iceberg salad with fruit, 24
    Endive and mushroom salad, 28
    Carrot salad with walnuts, 54
    Fruit salad with liqueur
        sauce, 66

Orange
  California salad, 6
  Spinach salad with oranges, 10
  Iceberg salad, 12
  Iceberg salad with fruit, 24
  Lamb's lettuce or endive salad
    Düsseldorf, 34
  Iceberg lettuce salad Thessa, 36
  Colourful vitamin salad, 54
  Savoury fennel salad, 61
  Fine fruit salad, 64
  Fruit salad with liqueur sauce, 66
  Kiwifruit salad, 70
  Fruit salad, 74
  Morning salad with avocado, 76

Pomegranate sauce, 89

Radish
  Chicory salad with horseradish, 7
  Summer salad, 20
  Salad with cream cheese
    dressing, 26
  Spinach salad, 30
  Mushroom, radish, endive
    medley, 32
  Iceberg salad with mango, 36
  Tomato with black radish sauce, 40
  Spring symphony, 42
  Salad potpourri, 44
  Summer watercress salad, 44
  Black radish spiral, 52
  Spring salad with egg, 52
  Radish salad, 56
  Cucumber salad with black
    radish, 60
  Cocktail dressing, 81

Raspberries
  Special melon fruit salad, 65

Berry salad with sekt zabaglione, 70
Iced grapes, 68
Berries with strawberry cream, 72
Berry salad, 72

Strawberries
  Berry dish, 64
  Strawberry dessert, 66
  Fruit salad Sabra, 68
  Kiwifruit salad, 70
  Berry salad, 72
  Fruit salad, 74
  Melon cocktail, 76
  Morning salad with avocado, 76

Spring turnip and carrot salad, 50

Sweetcorn salad, 22

Tomatoes
  Spanish salad, 16
  Salad with cream cheese dressing, 26
  Spinach salad, 30
  Cucumber tomato salad, 40
  Tomatoes with black radish sauce, 40
  Seville style tomatoes, 46
  "Nouvelle cuisine" salad, 48
  Andalusian salad, 50
  Spring salad with egg, 52
  Tomato salad, 60

Vinaigrette, 82

Watercress
  Watercress salad, 12
  Mushroom, radish, endive
    medley, 32
  Cucumber tomato salad, 40
  Summer watercress salad, 44
  Avocados with caper dressing, 56

ISBN 1-85129-030-3
Printed in Belgium.